COULD A MONKEY WATERSKI?

...and other questions

Aleksei Bitskoff &
Camilla de la Bédoyère

QEB

Capuchin monkeys are clever animal...

Design: Duck Egg Blue
Editor: Carly Madden
Editorial Director: Victoria Garrard
Art Director: Laura Roberts-Jensen
Publisher: Maxime Boucknooghe

Copyright © QEB Publishing 2016

First published in the United States in 2016 by
Part of the Quarto Group
QEB Publishing
6 Orchard
Lake Forest
CA 92630

www.qed-publishing.co.uk

A CIP record for this book is available from the Library of Congress.

ISBN 978 1 60992 945 9

Printed in China

hat live in the jungle.

They have mischievous faces, furry bodies, and long tails for gripping onto branches.

Imagine if a monkey came to stay. Would she have a fun time?

What if a monkey went into a Chinese restaurant?

She would eat **oodles of noodles.**

A monkey could use chopsticks because she has fingers and thumbs!

But she would cover her food with spiders, ants, and crabs. She loves eating crunchy bugs, fruit, seeds, and juicy green leaves in the jungle.

Would a monkey enjoy field day?

She would win the hurdles...

...and the long jump.

Monkeys can leap up to 10 feet when they are racing through trees.

That's like a human jumping more than 52 feet— or right over a bus!

Would a monkey enjoy bathtime?

Monkeys **love** water, so she'd have
a great time jumping into the bath!

SPLASH!

Monkeys often live in trees that grow alongside rivers, or the sea. When they get too hot they enjoy a cooling dip in the water.

SPLOSH!

Monkeys are great swimmers! They use their arms and legs to do the doggy-paddle.

Could a monkey help with the housework?

She could help to hang out the washing,

but she'd prefer to use the clothesline

o have some **fun!**

In the wild, monkeys swing from branch to branch. Each swing can carry them about ten feet.

She can even hang **upside down** using her strong tail.

Could a monkey waterski?

A monkey could waterski the **right way**...

...and the **wrong way!**

She can grip with her
feet as well as her hands
because her big toes
work like thumbs.

Would a monkey like to have her hair brushed?

No, she would prefer to have **smelly stuff** rubbed into it instead!

Insects often bite or sting monkeys, so monkeys cover themselves with squashed fruit and leaves, onions, mud, or bugs to keep the pests away.

Some monkeys even coat their fur **with pee!**

Would a monkey like to go to school?

She would **love** being in school.
Monkeys can learn, just like children!

Her favorite class would be **science**.

She would have fun
mixing colors,
stirring potions,
and making bubbles.

POP!

Monkeys are curious, smart animals. In the jungle, they like to explore, play, and discover new things.

Would a monkey have fun at the fair?

Yes, she would easily win a coconut at the ball toss booth.

In the jungle, monkeys sit in trees and throw **fruit, nuts,** and **branches** at animals below!

She would show everyone how
STRONG she is!

Monkeys use **big stones** to hit nuts and **CRACK** them open.

DING!

Would a monkey sleep in a bed?

No, she would sleep **on top of the wardrobe!**

In her jungle home she sleeps in the treetops, where she is safe from **big hungry animals**, such as jaguars and crocodiles!

She won't need a blanket because her **thick fur** will keep her warm.

But she might like a teddy bear to cuddle. Monkeys live in families, and they love **snuggly hugs!**

More about capuchin monkeys

Monkey is pointing to the place where she lives.
Can you see where you live?

FACT FILE

Capuchin monkeys live in trees and only come to the ground to drink water, grab food, or play.

Monkeys live in family groups, called troops. There can be 30 monkeys or more in a troop.

Capuchins can twitch their eyebrows to communicate their feelings!

Monkeys help the rainforest to grow. They eat fruits and the seeds pass through the monkeys' bodies, ready to start growing into plants and trees.

Monkeys have tails but apes (gorillas, chimps, and orangutans) are tailless.

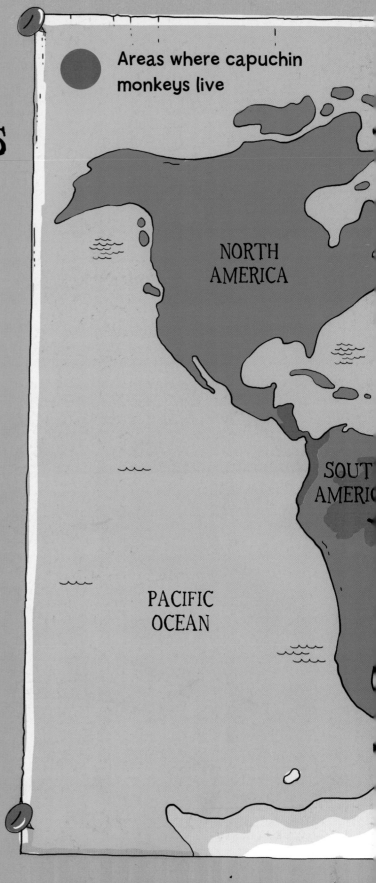

Areas where capuchin monkeys live

NORTH
AMERICA

SOUTH
AMERICA

PACIFIC
OCEAN

Greetings from South America!

POST CARD

I am writing this to you from the top of my favorite tree, looking over the river and watching a scary crocodile below! I have been throwing some nuts at him but he hasn't spotted me yet. Ha ha!

Come and visit me in the jungle some time.

Your best friend, Monkey   X

SENT BY CAPUCHIN POST
TREETOPS, BRAZIL

1ST

The Wild Family
189 Treetop Avenue
Chester, MO 12345

87132635605836745l9